Horace Mann

Horace Mann

OUR NATION'S FIRST EDUCATOR

EDITH GRAY PIERCE

Published by
Lerner Publications Company
Minneapolis, Minnesota

ACKNOWLEDGMENTS: The illustrations are reproduced through the courtesy of: p. 6, Library of Congress; pp. 9, 14, 16, 25, 36, 42, Independent Picture Service; pp. 10, 38, Dedham Historical Society; p. 12, A. Olsen, Franklin, Massachusetts; pp. 20-21, 22, Brown University; p. 28, George L. Banay Medical Library, Worcester State Hospital; p. 30, New York Academy of Medicine; p. 35, Cary Memorial Library, Lexington, Massachusetts; p. 44, The Corcoran Gallery of Art; p. 46, The Metropolitan Museum of Art, Gift of I. N. Phelps Stokes, Edward S. Hawes, Alice Mary Hawes, Marion Augusta Hawes, 1937; pp. 48, 51, 53, 54, Antioch College; front cover, Independent Picture Service; back cover, A. Olsen, Franklin, Massachusetts.

LIBRARY OF CONGRESS CATALOGING IN PUBLICATION DATA

Pierce, Edith Gray.
Horace Mann: our nation's first educator.

(The Real Life Books)
SUMMARY: A biography of the nineteenth-century lawyer who dedicated himself to reforming education in the United States.

1. Mann, Horace, 1796-1859—Juvenile literature. [1. Mann, Horace, 1796-1859. 2. Educators] I. Title.

LB695.M35P57   370'.924 [B] [92]   78-128805
ISBN 0-8225-0703-X

International Standard Book Number: 0-8225-0703-X
Library of Congress Catalog Card Number: 78-128805

Second Printing 1973

Contents

A one-room school of the late 18th century. There were few good public
schools in the United States during this period.

Introduction

There were very few schools in the United States 150 years ago. If a child's parents were rich, they hired a tutor to teach him reading, writing, spelling, and simple arithmetic. Often several children met at the teacher's house to be taught together. Because most of the teachers had also gone to inadequate schools, they knew little more than their pupils. Other children met in church and were taught by the minister. Their only school book was the Bible.

But if a child's parents were poor, he might never go to school at all. Instead, he had to work very hard. Some boys and girls worked on their families' farms, while others worked in mills and factories. They had little time to play. In fact, many children were forced to work such long hours that child labor laws were passed to set a limit to how long a boy or girl could work. In 1842 a law was passed in Massachusetts which said that children under 12 could work only 10 hours a day.

Occasionally some parents would get together to hire a teacher and organize a school. The schools they started were not very successful and never lasted very long. Schools in both Europe and the United States were poor. A report from England in 1843 described one school as having 40 children crammed together in a room 10 feet by 9 feet. Two hens and a rooster sat on a platform in the corner. A bed stood next to the wall, and underneath it was a dog kennel containing three black terriers who barked constantly. At the front of the room was one small window, but the teacher sat in front of it, blocking most of the light. Under these conditions it was very hard for children to study their lessons.

Conditions in the United States were just as bad. Some common schools did exist. Like our public schools of today, they were open to anyone. But they were cramped and uncomfortable. There were no maps, charts, or blackboards. In one Boston school of 400 students, there were about 65 whippings a day. Most of the school's windowpanes were broken and

A hornbook used in early American schools when bound books were scarce and expensive. A hornbook was a flat board with a handle. Fastened to it was a piece of paper on which was printed a school lesson. The board was covered with a thin sheet of clear horn, which protected the paper.

the floors were covered with mud.

Schools were in need of improvement. The United States was fortunate to find a man willing to dedicate his life to improving education. His name was Horace Mann.

Horace Mann, the father of the American public school system

1 A Man Named Horace

On May 4, 1796, a son, Horace, was born to Thomas and Rebecca Mann. With an older sister, Rebecca, two older brothers, Stanley and Stephen, and a younger sister, Lydia, he grew up on a farm near Franklin, Massachusetts.

As a boy, Horace loved to go to school. But he spent only about 10 weeks of every year in school because his family needed his help at home. Yet he went on to study at a university and to become a lawyer, a congressman, and then the president of a college. Because it had been so hard for him to get an education, Horace wanted to make it easier for other children to go to school. He did everything he possibly could to provide every child in Massachusetts with a good education in a free public school. His efforts inspired the rest of the nation to work toward the same

This monument marks the birthplace of Horace Mann in the town of Franklin, Massachusetts.

goal. A monument stands on the State House grounds in Boston, Massachusetts, in memory of his work. It was built with money donated by his friends and by the school children of the United States.

But Horace Mann also worked to improve other conditions in society. His efforts helped to provide treatment for the insane, change debtors' laws, and abolish slavery. He often asked the question "When will society, like a mother, take care of *all* her children?" But he didn't wait for someone else to give him an answer—he answered it himself by working to change and improve conditions for men, women, and children in the United States.

2 Boyhood

When Horace Mann was growing up, his family had little money and everyone had to work hard. Only by finishing their farm work early did the children have time to play. When they went to school, they had to buy their own books. They earned book money by braiding straw for a small factory in Franklin that made straw hats and bonnets.

Horace hated to braid straw. He found it dull and preferred to read. His sister Lydia offered to do his braiding. In exchange, Horace taught her to spell. Many afternoons were spent with Horace striding back and forth across the room, drilling Lydia on the importance of "i before e except after c," while she braided the straw.

On Sundays the Mann family did no work. Instead, they all went to church. They thought it

Horace Mann's boyhood home in Franklin, Massachusetts

was wrong to do any work on the Sabbath, so each Saturday they cooked enough food to last them through Sunday.

Most of Horace's early education came from the reading he did in the Franklin Public Library. At that time there were only about 10 or 12 libraries in the whole state of Massachusetts. The people of Franklin were very proud of their library. It had been donated by Benjamin Franklin because this town was the first in the United States to name itself after him. There were only 116 books in the library, but most of the libraries of that day were small. Books, also, were different from those we have today. They contained no colored pictures or interesting stories. Many of them were copies of speeches made by famous men years before.

Horace's father was the treasurer of the Franklin library. He wanted his children to have a good education, so he urged them to read the books. Horace read every history book in the library, but he stayed away from the sermons.

His father's health started to fail when Horace was 13. This year the cold caught by Thomas Mann every spring was not cured by the warm summer weather. Fearing that he would not live very long, he made plans for his children's futures: the oldest boy, Stanley, was to take care of his mother; Stephen, who was very smart, was to receive money for schooling; Horace was to continue to work hard, help his brothers, and take care of his mother and sisters. He was left one-quarter of the farm. The lawyer seemed very important as he read the will to the family. Horace was impressed. He decided that farm work was too hard, and that it would be a fine thing to be a lawyer. Shortly after his affairs were settled, Thomas Mann passed away.

There was only enough money to send one child to college, and that child had to be Stephen. Horace dutifully tended to his farm chores, but he still read in his spare time.

Stephen Mann was full of life and liked to have fun. Sometimes he stayed away from church and went swimming. His father never liked this. He wanted his

The Mann family attended the Franklin Congregational church every Sunday. There they heard the stern sermons of the Reverend Nathaniel Emmons.

children to do what he thought was right. "Stephen," he said, "you must always go to church on Sunday. It is wrong to play on the Lord's day."

But Stephen did not remember his words. One Sunday he was not in church. Before the service was over, a boy came running into the church crying out that Stephen Mann had drowned in the pond.

The Reverend Nathaniel Emmons had often preached on the evils of skipping church. Now he took the opportunity to preach against "Sabbath breakers." He declared that anyone who broke the Sabbath would, with Stephen Mann, be "damned for the glory of God." This was no consolation for the mother and her children. Instead, the pastor's words frightened them and they were heartsick. Horace Mann never forgot this sermon. It was not until many years later that he was finally able to free himself from this terrifying picture of God's justice.

With his father and brother gone, Horace had to help with the heavier farm chores. It was hard work. While he hoed weeds in the cornfield or drove cows to and from the pasture, Horace recited speeches. Some he had memorized from books in the town library. Others were speeches he made up himself.

Many of the speeches in the library books had been written by lawyers. Horace remembered the lawyer who had read his father's will and decided he would like to study law. But to do that, he had to go to college. To go to college, he had to know Latin and Greek, and there was no one in Franklin to teach him.

One day a man wandered into Franklin. The townspeople reported that he was a drunkard who had no home. He could not even tell time. But he knew Latin and Greek. Horace heard about him and hunted all over town until he found him. "Would you teach me?" Horace asked. "I want to go to college."

"I fear I cannot teach you," Samuel Barrett answered. "I know nothing of mathematics. I know Latin and Greek backwards and forwards, but I cannot even add numbers."

"But it is Latin and Greek I must know," Horace said. "If you can help me learn to read Latin and Greek and to know the grammar, I can get into college."

"Very well," replied the man. "I will come to your house every day and teach you."

Horace studied with him for six months. At the end of that time he knew Latin and Greek well enough to pass the college exams.

3 The University

Horace was 20 years old when he took the stage-coach to Providence, Rhode Island, to enter Brown University. He immediately took oral and written tests. He did so well that he started college as a sophomore. Tuition was $20 a term, and board was less than $2 a week. His father had provided that, should Stephen Mann not go to college, the money should go to Horace. But it didn't amount to much. Horace knew he would have to budget his money carefully to stay in school long enough to graduate. Since it would take only three years, he was sure he could do it.

At school he was invited to join a club named the United Brothers. It was an oratory club in which the members took turns debating different topics. A popular subject was government policy. One time Horace was on the affirmative side for the topic "Is

Brown University in the early 1800s, when Horace Mann was a student there

it politic for the Republic of the United States to establish military schools?" His team won. They switched sides, and again Horace's side won. Again and again Horace proved that he was the best speaker of his class.

In his senior year he was elected vice president,

lecturer, and then president of his class. At graduation
Horace was chosen to be speaker at the Examination
Dinner for the senior class. It was the highest honor any
student could receive. In his speech Horace said that
"education should reach like a ladder from earth to
heaven."

Charlotte Messer Mann, Horace Mann's first wife

4 Beginning of a Career

Horace still wanted to be a lawyer. After graduation he took a job in a law office. His work was to write
and copy legal papers. In his spare time Horace read
law books. One day he received a letter from Asa
Messer, president of Brown University. Dr. Messer had
not forgotten his good student. He wanted Horace to
come back to Brown University to teach.

At first Horace agreed to go and teach for two
years. Then he changed his mind. If he took a teaching
job, he might never become a lawyer. Again Dr. Messer
asked him to come to Brown. Horace finally accepted.
He taught a class of 40 freshmen boys. Many of his
students were full of mischief, but Horace could handle
them. Some became his friends for life.

During his own school days Horace had often
visited the home of Asa Messer. Now that he was

teaching, he continued his visits. The Messers had three daughters. When Horace first met them, Mary was 21, Caroline was 15, and Charlotte was 12. Charlotte was very lovely, and Horace liked her the best. When he left Brown, he could not forget her.

When his teaching job ended, Horace went to Connecticut to enter Litchfield Law School, the first law school established in the United States. Once again he burned the midnight oil studying long and hard. When he finished in the spring of 1823, he entered a law office in Dedham, Massachusetts, a town of about 100 houses.

Horace was now 27 years old, and he still liked to make speeches. He was pleased when the citizens of Dedham asked him to give the oration at their big Fourth of July celebration. He prepared his speech carefully and then was almost unable to give it. On June 14, his face was strangely swollen—he had the mumps! But he got well just in time to give the speech. Everyone who heard it liked it. Later he was elected Dedham's representative to the state legislature in Boston.

Horace had not forgotten the youngest daughter of Asa Messer. On June 9, 1829, he wrote a letter to

The State House in Boston, Massachusetts, where Horace Mann served as a representative of the town of Dedham

Charlotte proposing marriage. He had written other letters to her, but she had never answered them. Horace was certain she would answer his proposal. He waited and waited. No letter came. He wrote her a second letter, beginning it "My dearest Miss Charlotte." Again he received no answer. Several days later he traveled to Providence to find out why she didn't write. Charlotte told him that she liked him very much. But her parents felt that she should not write to any man unless she was engaged to marry him. Because she was young—only 20 years old—they felt she should take her time deciding whether or not to accept Mr. Mann's proposal. It would not be proper for her to write to him until she decided to marry him.

The next time Horace called on her in Providence, Charlotte promised to marry him. Although she didn't care much for writing letters, she finally wrote to him, beginning her letter "My Friend." Horace's reply began "My dearest, loveliest Charlotte."

When she married Horace that autumn, Charlotte was 21 years old. She had always been frail, but Horace was sure that she would become healthy and strong under his care. He watched over her carefully, but the winter that year was severe—snowdrifts were piled eight feet high. The cold was too much for Charlotte and she became ill. She was forced to remain in Dedham while Horace worked in the legislature in Boston.

With Charlotte's support Horace felt capable of doing anything, but he was lonely in Boston without her. Charlotte went through a series of illnesses and recoveries. Finally, in the spring of 1832, she seemed totally well. At last she was able to work on chores and projects around the house. The months of May and June were especially happy for Charlotte and Horace that year. They spent much time together outdoors, strolling up and down the streets of Dedham. But at the end of June, Charlotte again took sick. On July 31, as Horace was watching over her, she died. Horace stayed with her until the next morning when the doctor arrived. Charlotte was buried in the Messer family plot at North Burying Grounds in Providence.

Horace did not recover quickly from Charlotte's death. It had been a great shock to him. Shortly after her funeral he left Dedham for good.

The Worcester State Lunatic Hospital, around 1850. Horace Mann persuaded the Massachusetts state legislature to build this hospital, one of
the first of its kind in the United States.

5 Schools for Everyone

When Horace gave up his residence in Dedham, he also had to give up his seat in the state legislature. He returned to the practice of law, but he continued his work for the insane. Horace had persuaded the Massachusetts legislature to give funds for the building of a state hospital. It was to be one of the first hospitals for the insane in the country. Up to this time the insane had been kept in dirty jails, often in chains, and had been clothed in rags and fed on leftovers. Horace was made head of a committee set up to supervise the building of the new hospital. He saw that both builders and suppliers were trying to cheat the state on expenses. The builders tried to use defective lumber, but Horace discovered it and made them replace it with good lumber. He also made certain that the workers were not drunk on the job.

During the 1800s, mental illness was treated by the use of devices such as this "tranquillizing chair." Horace Mann worked hard to improve the care given to the mentally ill in Massachusetts.

Finally the Worcester State Lunatic Hospital was finished, and patients were admitted. The good air, balanced meals, warm rooms, and clean facilities helped create a pleasant atmosphere. As a result, many of the worst-behaved patients became quiet and manageable. Horace was later appointed commissioner of the hospital, and from 1833 to 1838 he served as a trustee, writing the hospital's annual reports.

Horace also worked to change debtors' laws. A man could be put in jail for owing someone as little as 68 cents. In 1828 more than 75,000 citizens of the United States were in jail for not being able to pay money they owed. Most of the debts were less than $20. Once a man was put in jail, he had no way of getting money to repay the debt. Horace felt that the laws were too harsh and he tried to get them changed.

In 1837, five years after Charlotte's death, Horace was urged to accept the position of secretary of the Massachusetts Board of Education. Although it meant he would have to give up his law practice, he accepted. Immediately he returned to Franklin to study, reading everything that he could find about education. Then he began to visit common schools throughout the state to see for himself what improvements were needed.

In each town and village he visited, Horace gave a speech. One time he had to sweep out the school room himself before giving his speech. At first his audiences were small. But interest grew, and more and more people came to hear him speak. Some people argued that the present schools were good enough. To them,

Horace replied, "Nothing is so good it cannot be made better—nothing so bad it might not become worse. . . ."

On January 1, 1838, Horace read the first report of his findings to the State Board of Education. As secretary, he made a total of 12 annual reports. Horace usually made suggestions for improving the schools of Massachusetts. He had to persuade the people that education was important. Schools, he said, should be free, so that everyone could attend.

Finally Horace's efforts began to get results. People voted to have their schools regularly inspected to keep them in good condition. They decided that books used in school should be carefully selected and that children too poor to buy their own books should be given them free of charge.

Next Horace campaigned to provide books and libraries for the common schools. He searched for satisfactory books. They had to be approved by every member of the school board. One book that Horace reviewed was about a young boy who had done some mischief. The book described how he would be punished—his body would be "wrapped in a shroud, placed in the coffin, and buried in the grave," while someone read the words "Depart from me into everlasting fire!" The book reminded Horace of the terrifying sermon Dr. Emmons had preached the day Stephen Mann died. He refused to have such a book in one of his libraries. Another book from the same publisher told how wicked little children were punished. This, too, Horace refused to buy for his libraries, explaining that it was unlawful. A law passed in 1827 guaranteed religious freedom to public schools, which meant that no religious books could be used in school. There followed much argument between the publishers of the books and the Board of Education members, but the issue was finally settled in Horace's favor—the books were not bought.

Horace also worked for the improvement of school buildings. Most school rooms were too small for the number of pupils in them, they were either too hot or too cold, depending on how close one sat to the heater, and the roofs leaked. (Luckily the floors leaked too and the water drained out instead of filling up the room.) Horace said that children who disliked attending such schools should not be whipped. Instead, their parents should be whipped for not providing better schools.

In addition to the grammar schools, public high

schools were being built so that students could continue their education. Boston was the first town to start a high school. At first only boys were admitted, but in 1826 a high school for girls was opened. So many girls applied for admission to this school that conditions became overcrowded, and the mayor closed the school. Some people still didn't seem to understand the need to educate everyone.

But learning depends on more than just books and school buildings. In order for students to learn, they must have teachers who know how to teach them. Horace began working for the establishment of "normal schools," which would train teachers to teach school. This, he felt, was even more important than providing books for school libraries. Teachers needed to know their subjects well so they could teach them effectively. They also needed to be trained in teaching methods. Again Horace traveled from schoolhouse to schoolhouse trying to convince people of the importance of starting normal schools. He accused them of spending more money to improve their cattle than they spent to improve their children.

Lexington, Massachusetts, was chosen to be the site of the first normal school. It opened July 3, 1839.

The school accepted only those students who wanted to be teachers. They had to be at least 16 years old, in good health, and of good moral character. Tuition was free, but pupils had to pay for their own board, books, and other expenses. Only three girls came to school the first day, but by the end of the year there

The Lexington Normal School was the first school in Massachusetts established to train teachers.

Cyrus Peirce

were about 25 students. Most of them had been poorly taught—many could hardly read or spell, but they soon learned.

Cyrus Peirce, an educator from Nantucket, was asked to be the school's principal. He ran it so successfully that in the next two years, two more normal schools were opened.

In this first normal school the students tried to find answers to familiar teaching problems. Some of the questions they discussed were: "How can we make the school so delightful a place that even the truants will come?" "What shall we say to a pupil who prompts another during recitation?" "How can we help the lad who copies his work from another?" They also were taught not to hit school children. Horace believed that "to thwack a child over the head because he doesn't get his lesson, is about as wise as it would be to rap a watch with a hammer because it does not keep good time."

Horace continued his yearly tours of the Massachusetts schools, urging people to support the cause of education. His slogan was "Teach the People." He also made the yearly reports to the Board of Education and started a magazine called the *Common School Journal*. In the journal he wrote of the progress of schools and explained his philosophy of education. Also included were lessons to be used by teachers in their classes. When there was space available in the magazine, Horace sometimes added a lighter touch by including a brief thought of his own. In one issue he wrote: "Lost yesterday, somewhere between sunrise and sunset, *two golden hours,* each set with *sixty diamond minutes.* No reward is offered for they are gone forever."

In 1843, Horace Mann married Mary Peabody, an old friend from Boston.

6 A Family

Horace Mann was described as being of striking appearance and radiant personality. Slender and erect, he stood over six feet tall. He had sparkling eyes and a resonant voice. His hair had turned gray at an early age and he cut quite a dashing figure. He was kind and affectionate, and he loved children. It is no wonder that Mary Peabody had long admired him. She first met Horace while living with her sisters, Elizabeth and Sophia, at Mrs. Clarke's boarding house in Boston. After Charlotte's death Horace had gone to Boston to practice law, and he boarded at the same place. The sisters and Horace became close friends and spent many hours discussing Horace's favorite subject— education. After they had each moved to other parts of the country, they continued their discussions by letter.

Horace knew that Mary Peabody had long wanted to teach school. After he became secretary of the Board of Education, he arranged for her to return to Boston to interview for a teaching position in a new school. Elizabeth Peabody had opened a book shop in the city, and Mary helped in her sister's shop while waiting for the new school to open. She also tutored students in her home and found time to write and publish a book called *Flower People*.

Mary was happy in Boston and enjoyed her work. She liked living there because she was near Horace and might bump into him on the street at any time. She was as interested in education as he was and helped him with his school reports. Horace often sent out questionnaires to towns, asking about school conditions. Mary counted up the results from these questionnaires and gave them to Horace, who added the information to his reports. She also wrote the school lessons published in Horace's *Common School Journal*.

On March 26, 1843, Horace became engaged to Mary Tyler Peabody. It was a happy occasion for both of them. The memory of Charlotte was still very dear to Horace, but he no longer felt the sharp pain of her absence. He wanted to be part of a family once again. For many years Mary Peabody had secretly hoped to become Mrs. Horace Mann. She didn't have to hope any longer.

The Manns planned to travel to Germany on their honeymoon, but it wasn't to be a pleasure trip. While there, Horace wanted to observe the European schools. Mary immediately began to study with a German tutor in preparation for the trip.

They looked at schools in England, Ireland, Scotland, Holland, Germany, and France. But in six months they were homesick for the United States and sailed home. They took lodgings in Boston and Horace started work on his seventh annual report. This 1843 report has since proved to be his most famous. It started much controversy, for in it Horace wrote of his findings in Europe. He praised the teaching methods of the German schools and suggested that Massachusetts schools were inferior. The people of Massachusetts did not like having their schools criticized, and a bitter argument developed.

The controversy over Horace's seventh annual school report continued during the following year. In 1844 the Manns also had their first child, a son whom they named Horace. It is reported that his father found

Horace and Mary Mann had three sons. Horace Jr. (center) was born in 1844, George (right) in 1846, and Benjamin (left) in 1848.

him perfect in every detail. Another son, George, was born in January 1846. The Mann family was growing. Mary and Horace had been content to live in rented quarters when there were just the two of them, but children needed a house and room to play. So Horace bought some land in West Newton, a town about 10 miles from Boston, and had a house built for his family. On Christmas Eve, 1846, the Manns moved to their new home.

Although West Newton had a population of only 1,000, it was one of the few towns that could boast of having a normal school. Horace was happy living there. The pressure of his work did not seem as great as it had in the city, and he was able to relax and spend some time with his family. He played with his children and told them stories. He disapproved of fairy tales, but he told them many stories of science and nature.

Horace wrote his 12th and last annual report as Board of Education secretary in 1848. This report summarized his other reports and repeated some of his theories on education. He wrote that it was necessary for schools to provide physical training for their pupils (Horace's own health had been poor since his college days, so he always emphasized the importance of good health). Some of his other ideas were that students should be grouped in classes, that school attendance should be compulsory, that pupils should be taught to think rather than to memorize, that music should be taught, and that it was important for students to experience success rather than failure in their work. The group of 12 reports contains every idea that has become part of the American philosophy of education.

Until 1857, the United States House of Representatives met in this impressive chamber in the Capitol. Horace Mann served here as a representative from 1848 to 1852.

7 Serving the Cause of Freedom

Horace had worked hard to improve the schools of Massachusetts, but now he had another job to do. In February 1848, John Quincy Adams, former president of the United States, was stricken with paralysis and died soon afterwards. He had been serving in the United States Congress as a representative. Now a replacement was needed. People remembered Horace Mann's work in the Massachusetts legislature and chose him to fill the vacancy. They felt that Horace shared John Quincy Adams' devotion to the principles of human freedom.

But Horace hesitated to accept the nomination. He was still deeply involved in his work for schools. He also felt that he could never take Mr. Adams' place—he said that it was "like asking a mouse to fill the skin of an elephant." Finally he was persuaded to

John Quincy Adams had a long and distinguished career of public service. When he died in 1848, Horace Mann took his place in the House of Representatives. *(Courtesy, The Metropolitan Museum of Art)*

accept, and on April 3, 1848, he was elected to serve the rest of Mr. Adams' term of office. The following month he resigned as secretary of the Board of Education.

As a representative, Horace worked hard for the causes he supported. One of these was the abolition of slavery. He thought that liberty was the right of every man. On June 30, 1848, he gave a speech in the House on the subject of slavery in the territories. In it he said that slaves are made to work from fear, and that slavery destroys a man's ambitions.

In July Horace had a chance to do more for the cause of abolition than make speeches. A man named Daniel Drayton was to be tried in court for stealing 70 Negro slaves from the District of Columbia and helping them to escape. This was not the first time that Captain Drayton had used the schooner *Pearl* to help slaves escape to free states. This time, however, he had been caught and put in jail along with the owner of the schooner. Horace Mann consented to defend them. He felt he was defending not only the two men but also the "whole colored race." He poured all his energies into his defense. Finally Horace won a victory of sorts. Each man was given a fine of $1,000 and released.

Running for the Free Soil Party, Horace was elected to Congress from the 8th District two more times. In 1852 the party nominated him for governor of Massachusetts. He lost to the Whig party candidate. Horace was almost glad he lost, for he had another project in mind.

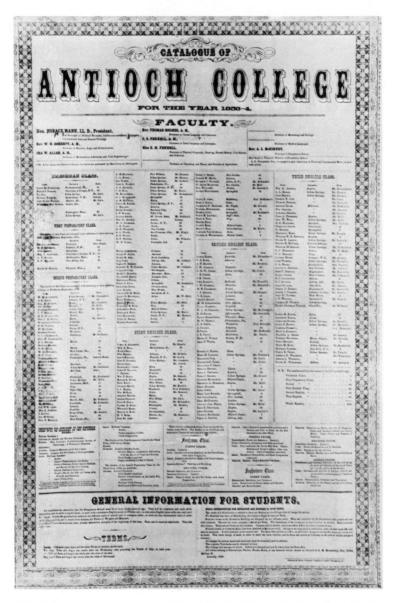

The first school catalog issued by Antioch College. In keeping with the school's policy, the catalog states that "equal opportunities for education are offered both sexes."

8 A School of His Own

Two months before the election, Horace had heard about plans for a new college. It was to be built by a church group called the Christian church. The small village of Yellow Springs, Ohio, was chosen to be the site of the college, which was to be named Antioch. The church members wanted to have a president who was well known and respected. No one was better known for work with schools than Horace Mann, so they asked Horace to serve as president. Horace was not a member of the Christian denomination but, as a Unitarian, he shared many of their beliefs. To be a member of the Christian church one had only to live a Christian life.

Horace was 56 years old, but he did not mind moving to a new home in a new part of the country. Yellow Springs could not offer him the life of culture that he enjoyed in Boston but, according to Horace, the area was one of the most beautiful on earth. His new job was a challenge, and Horace had always liked challenges. He looked forward to the Ohio move, but when it finally came time to leave Boston, he wept.

Antioch College was a college for both men and women. In the East, men and women went to separate schools. Some educators thought that women were not as smart as men. But Horace knew that this was not true. He knew that both sexes were of equal intelligence, and he thought that they should have the same opportunities. At Antioch men and women had an equal right to a good education.

The college was officially opened October 5, 1853. More than 3,000 people came to take part in the festivities. Many had come to hear the famous educator Horace Mann speak. He dedicated Antioch College to "the honor of God and the service of man."

The 150 students entering that first year were both young and old. Many of them were housewives, farmers, and ministers. When the college opened, the buildings were not finished. According to college records, there were no fireplaces or stoves, no books in the library and no shelves to put them on, no school

The campus of Antioch College during Horace Mann's term as president. The building on the right is Antioch Hall. South Hall (left), a men's dormitory, was under construction when this photograph was taken.

chairs, no blackboards, and no desks. The examinations for new students were given in the dining room, and whenever it was time for a meal, pencils and papers had to be cleared away. There were no fences around the college buildings, no doors to the halls, and no special pens for the animals, so the Ohio pigs walked through the dining room. Students walking across campus had to carry a shingle along to scrape off mud from the bottoms of their shoes. Sometimes it would get so thick that they couldn't walk any further. But in spite of the difficulties, those connected with the college were certain that it would soon be a fine institution.

Horace was a good administrator. He believed that kindness and trust were more effective in disciplining the students than the use of punishment. The good behavior of his students proved that Horace was right.

The first years were hard ones, however. Antioch managed to stay open, but in 1857 the country was entering a time of financial stress. Factories were closed, businesses were ruined, and railroads were going broke. The construction of Antioch was still not completed when prices for building materials rose. The college was soon in debt. Horace's health also suffered, but he continued his work.

Finally Antioch had to be sold to pay some of the bills. Friends of the college bought it and kept it going. The college was saved. At the 1859 graduation exercises, Horace gave a stirring speech to the assembly. He urged the graduating seniors to carry on a march for the welfare of man. He concluded by saying "... I beseech you to treasure up in your hearts these my parting words: Be ashamed to die until you have won some victory for humanity."

At the age of 63 Horace had already fought and won his battles, and now he was tired. He burned with fever and day by day grew weaker. On August 2, 1859, he met with family and friends for the last time. He urged them, above all, to obey God's laws.

Antioch College today. Antioch Hall (left) and South Hall are still part of the campus scene.

A statue of Horace Mann on the campus of Antioch College

He was buried on the grounds of Antioch College, but the following year Mary Mann had his remains taken to North Burying Grounds in Providence, Rhode Island. There he was buried next to his first wife, Charlotte.

The schools of today owe a great deal to Horace Mann. His efforts made it possible for every child in the United States to receive a good education at a free public school. This was his victory for humanity.

The Real Life Books

WILL ROGERS
The Cowboy Who Walked With Kings

HORACE MANN
Our Nation's First Educator

GREAT INVENTIONS

HOW MEN DISCOVERED THE WORLD

HUNTERS OF THE BLACK SWAMP

THE PROUDEST HORSE ON THE PRAIRIE

We specialize in publishing quality books for
young people. For a complete list please write

LERNER PUBLICATIONS COMPANY
241 First Avenue North, Minneapolis, Minnesota 55401